Young Environmental HEROES

Adam Ford

Young Environmental Heroes

Text: Adam Ford
Publishers: Tania Mazzeo and Eliza Webb
Series consultant: Amanda Sutera
Hands on Heads Consulting
Editor: Kirstie Innes-Will
Project editor: Annabel Smith
Designer: Leigh Ashforth
Project designer: Danielle Maccarone
Permissions researchers: Lumina Datamatics
Production controller: Renee Tome

Acknowledgements
We would like to thank the following for permission to reproduce copyright material:

Front cover: Alistair Berg/DigitalVision/Getty Images; p. 5: (top) Teo Tarras/Shutterstock.com; (bottom) totajla/Shutterstock.com; p. 6: Sambulov Yevgeniy/Shutterstock.com; p. 8: (top right) iStock.com/naumoid; (top middle) iStock.com/SeanXu; (top left) iStock.com/DariuszPa; (bottom left) iStock.com/Maxiphoto; (bottom right) nagelestock.com/Alamy Stock Photo; p. 9: Ashley Cooper pics/Alamy Stock Photo; p. 10: Imago/Alamy Stock Photo; p. 11: iStock.com/Schroptschop; p. 12: iStock.com/zetter; p. 13: (top) thelamephotographer/Shutterstock.com; (bottom) Diyana Dimitrova/Shutterstock.com; p. 14: Liv Oeian/Shutterstock.com; p. 15: picture alliance/picture alliance/Getty Images; p. 16: ARphotography/Alamy Stock Photo; p. 17: (top) iStock.com/primeimages; (bottom) Marta V/Shutterstock.com; p. 18: (top) William Robinson/Alamy Stock Photo; (bottom) Abaca Press/Alamy Stock Photo; p. 19: (top) PETER PARKS/AFP/Getty Images; (bottom) ZUMA Press Inc/Alamy Stock Photo; p. 20: Guido Paradisi/Alamy Stock Photo; p. 21: (top) Sergey Timofeev/Alamy Stock Photo; (bottom) iStock.com/Frederick Doerschem; p. 22; (back cover): Drazen_/E+/Getty Images; p. 23: Philip Schubert/Shutterstock.com; p. 24: Viktor Sergeevich/Shutterstock.com; p. 25: (top) SanderMeertinsPhotography/Shutterstock.com; (bottom) Kostiantyn Kravchenko/Alamy Stock Photo; p. 26: (top) Kristian Bell/Shutterstock.com; (bottom) Horia Bogdan/Shutterstock.com; p. 27: Ali A Suliman/Shutterstock.com; p. 28: Stefan Cristian Cioata/Moment/Getty Images; p. 29: (top) LDNPix/Alamy Stock Photo; (bottom) (title page) Sutthichai Supapornpasupad/Moment/Getty Images; p. 30: (top) iStock.com/SolStock; (bottom) iStock.com/Wavebreakmedia.

Every effort has been made to trace and acknowledge copyright. However, if any infringement has occurred, the publishers tender their apologies and invite the copyright holders to contact them.

NovaStar

ISBN 978 0 17 033517 1

Cengage Learning Australia
Level 5, 80 Dorcas Street
Southbank VIC 3006 Australia
Phone: 1300 790 853
Email: aust.nelsonprimary@cengage.com

For learning solutions, visit **cengage.com.au**

Printed in China by 1010 Printing International Ltd
1 2 3 4 5 6 7 29 28 27 26 25

Nelson acknowledges the Traditional Owners and Custodians of the lands of all First Nations Peoples. We pay respect to Elders past and present, and extend that respect to all First Nations Peoples today.

Contents

Facing Climate Change

Do you know what **climate change** is and how it is affecting our environment? Many young people are concerned about how climate change will influence their future.

It can be alarming when you read headlines such as these:

The ice caps at the North and South Poles are melting.

The air is polluted.

The great forests such as the Amazon are being cut down.

Many animals are facing extinction.

But it's not all bad news. We can reduce the threats that climate change poses, and we can take action to protect our environment.

What Is Climate?

Climate is the pattern of weather, such as temperature or rainfall, in a particular area over a long time. Climate patterns are different around the world. For example, the climate in areas closer to the **equator** is generally hot and rainy. As you move closer to the North or South Poles, temperatures are lower and there are clear differences in weather at different times of the year. We call these seasons.

Weather versus Climate

"Climate" describes conditions over a long period of time. "Weather" is the specific conditions on a particular day.

Tropical rainforests and deserts have very different climates.

What Is Climate Change and What Is Global Warming?

Climate change is a change in climate patterns over a long period of time. For the last two centuries, Earth's climate has been changing much faster than before, due to human activities. This is what people usually mean when they talk about "climate change" or "the climate emergency".

Climate change and global warming can lead to flooding in coastal areas.

Scientists have observed that Earth's climate is getting warmer overall. Some of the warmest years ever recorded have been in the last 20 years. This rise in global temperature is called "global warming".

What Causes Climate Change and Global Warming?

Some of the gases in Earth's **atmosphere** trap heat from the Sun – just like the glass roof and walls of a greenhouse do. These are called "greenhouse gases", and they keep Earth warm enough for humans, animals and plants to live on.

Fossil fuels, including petrol, coal and oil, are burned to create electricity, to heat our homes, to power our computers or as fuel for vehicles. These fossil fuels release extra greenhouse gases into the atmosphere, trapping even more of the Sun's heat and leading to a warmer Earth.

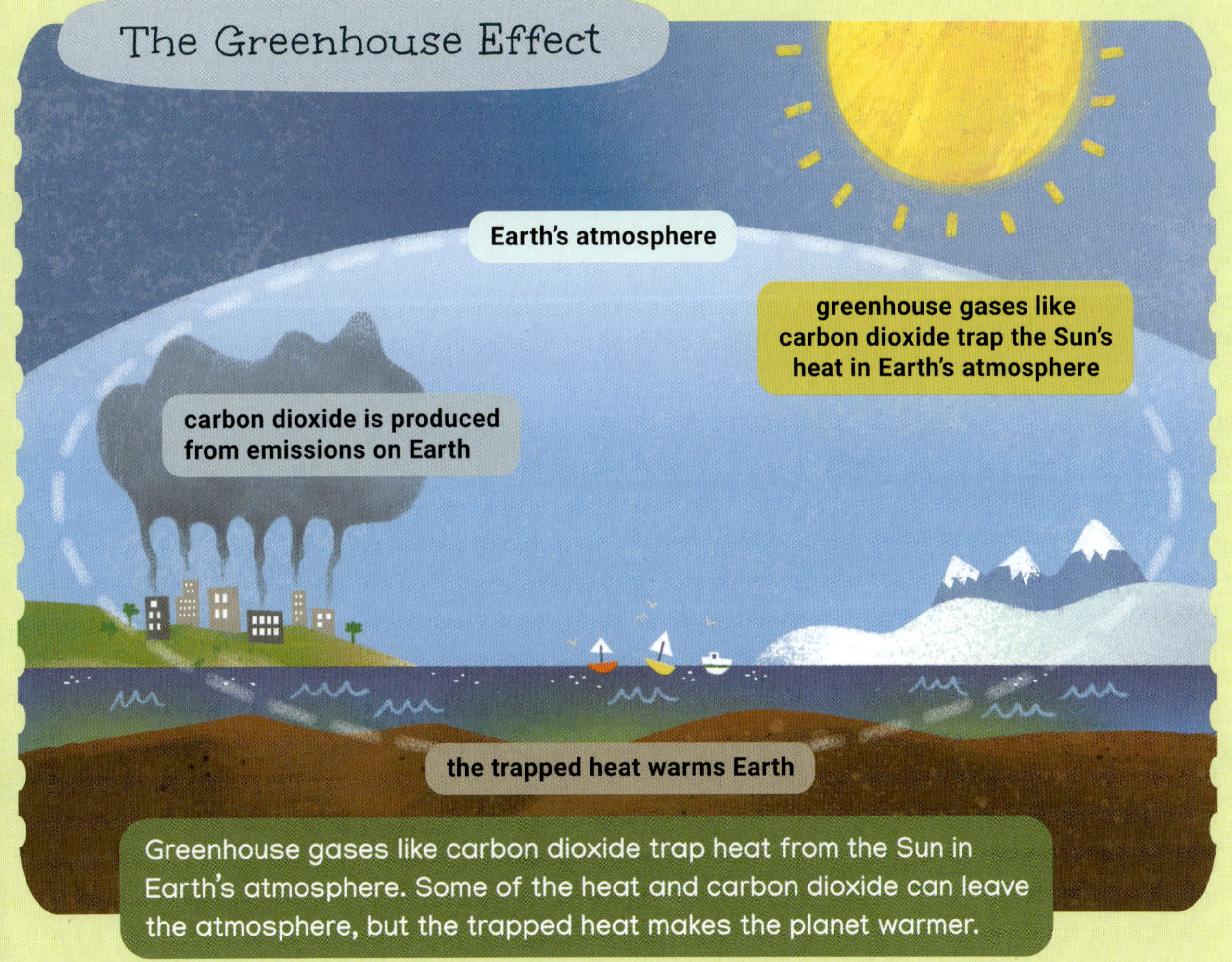

Greenhouse gases like carbon dioxide trap heat from the Sun in Earth's atmosphere. Some of the heat and carbon dioxide can leave the atmosphere, but the trapped heat makes the planet warmer.

The Environment

Climate is a part of the environment, which is made up of every natural thing in the world around us, including the air (also known as the atmosphere), water, land and living things (plants and animals).

Each part of the environment influences and affects the other parts. For example, the temperature of the sea affects the plants and animals that live in it. A healthy environment relies on maintaining a delicate balance between all the different parts.

The Five Aspects of our Environment

Why Is a Healthy Environment Important?

You might think Earth becoming warmer is a good thing if you don't like the cold. But rapid climate change disrupts the balance between the five aspects of our environment, creating problems. For example, as the temperature of the atmosphere increases, the seas warm up and ice sheets at the North and South Poles melt, which makes sea levels rise.

Most of the world's population lives near water. Sea levels rising make some areas unsafe to live in. This is a particularly big problem for people who live on small islands; if the ocean rises too high, these people will have nowhere to live.

The island nation of Tuvalu is at high risk of flooding as sea levels rise.

What Is Being Done About Climate Change?

Many people are working to encourage governments around the world to take action on climate change by reducing the burning of fossil fuels. The **United Nations** organises big conferences where people from countries all over the world gather to discuss what can be done about climate change.

If climate change continues, future generations will find it harder to live comfortably. Young people have a very important role to play in **advocating** for change and the importance of looking after our environment.

These children are protesting about climate change outside a United Nations conference.

Atmosphere

The atmosphere is made up of gases, including oxygen and carbon dioxide, that you cannot see or smell. All living things need clean air to survive and be healthy. Earth's atmosphere protects us from the Sun's harmful rays, including **ultraviolet (UV) light,** which causes sunburn.

Air pollution is caused by fumes from cars and trucks, and smoke from the burning of fossil fuels.

WHAT'S IN OUR AIR?

We need oxygen to breathe, but it only makes up 21 per cent of the air in our atmosphere. Most of the air (78 per cent) is nitrogen.

This coal-fired power station releases a lot of pollution into the atmosphere.

Burning fossil fuels releases a lot of carbon dioxide into the atmosphere. Carbon dioxide is a natural part of the air and is important for life on Earth – for instance, trees need to absorb carbon dioxide to live. But too much carbon dioxide in the atmosphere is causing Earth to warm more than usual.

Carbon dioxide in the atmosphere has increased by 50 per cent in the last 200 years. To help our atmosphere, we all need to do our part to reduce harmful air pollution **emissions**.

In a healthy environment, trees absorb carbon dioxide emissions, keeping everything in balance.

One way we can help our environment is by using less energy. For instance, we can turn off lights and appliances when we are not using them.

We can also change the kind of energy we use. Solar and wind power are forms of "renewable energy", which we can use instead of burning fossil fuels.

Wind turbines produce renewable energy.

Renewable Versus Non-Renewable Energy

Renewable energy comes from resources that nature will replace, or renew, such as sunshine, wind or water.

Non-renewable energy comes from resources that cannot be replaced once they are used up, such as fossil fuels.

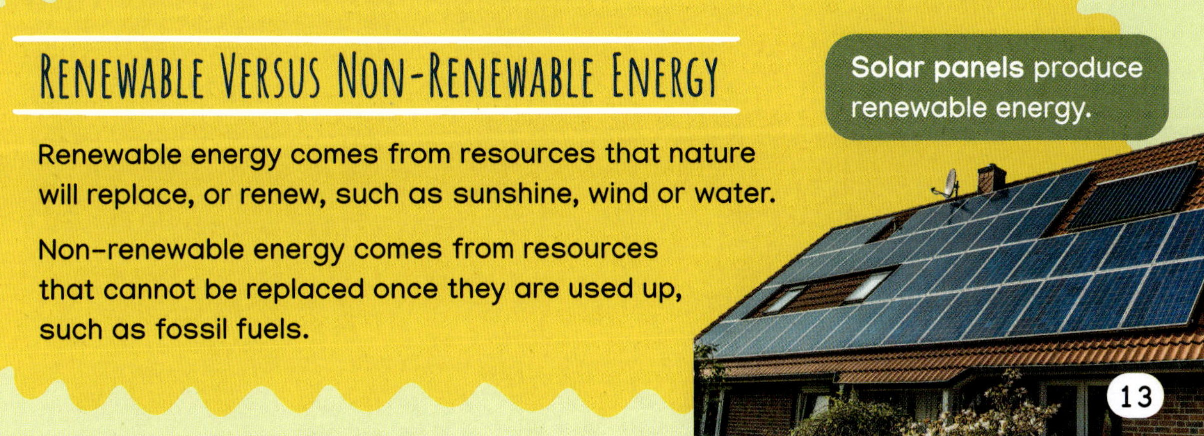

Solar panels produce renewable energy.

YOUNG ENVIRONMENTAL HERO:

Greta Thunberg

Once we start to act, hope is everywhere. So instead of looking for hope, look for action.

Greta Thunberg is one of the most famous young environmental heroes. When she was 15 years old, Greta started protesting about climate change outside the parliament in Sweden, where she lived. She felt the world's governments were not taking enough action.

With a handmade sign and determination, Greta launched a youth **movement** for climate action that spread all around the world. She inspired many other young people to join protests.

Greta protested every Friday outside the Swedish parliament from 2018 to 2019.

Greta was invited to speak at a meeting of the United Nations in New York, USA. She travelled there by boat to avoid flying, which uses a lot of fossil fuels. She told all the world leaders at the meeting that they had "stolen" her future – and the future of other young people – by prioritising **economic growth** over protecting Earth's environment. Greta urged world leaders to stop using fossil fuels as soon as possible.

Greta spoke to people protesting about the climate during meetings of the United Nations.

Water

Water makes up the seas, lakes and rivers that cover almost three-quarters of Earth's surface. These bodies of water are home to almost 250 000 species of animals, plants and **microorganisms**.

Water is also a part of weather. Clouds, rain, snow and the huge sheets of ice that cover the North and South Poles are water in different forms.

All living things need clean water. As well as drinking it, we use water to cook food, wash ourselves, grow crops and operate machinery.

When snow melts it flows from the mountains into the rivers, such as this crystal-clear river in Slovakia.

Clouds

Clouds are made up of **water vapour,** and the average cloud weighs about 1 million tonnes!

Global warming is changing patterns of rainfall and snowfall, and melting the polar **ice caps**. These changes are making many areas of the world harder to live in. It causes more frequent **droughts** in some areas and damaging floods in others.

Human activities are affecting the planet's water resources in other ways, too. Dumped chemicals and rubbish, particularly plastic waste, have polluted almost every water source in the world.

Poor water quality harms plants and animals. For example, water polluted with **sewage** can spread diseases, and water polluted with chemicals cannot be used to grow crops.

This waterway has been polluted with chemicals.

We can reduce how much water we use, particularly during times of drought. And we can help make sure our waterways are free of rubbish and polluting chemicals. But the most important way to look after our water resources is to limit climate change and slow global warming.

During a drought, we might have to follow instructions for when to use water, to avoid using up this precious resource.

Giant Garbage Patch

The South Pacific Garbage Patch is 1.6 million square kilometres (three times the size of France) of floating rubbish formed by swirling currents in the middle of the Pacific Ocean.

YOUNG ENVIRONMENTAL HEROES:

Pacific Climate Warriors

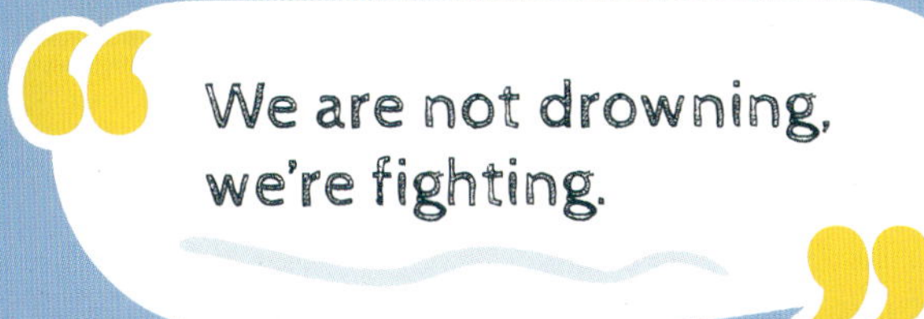

The Pacific Climate Warriors launched a campaign against the coal industry in Australia.

The Pacific Climate Warriors are a group of young people from 15 Pacific Island nations who work to highlight the consequences of climate change on their homelands. Many islands are already losing land to rising sea levels.

The Pacific Climate Warriors demand that pollution and greenhouse gas emissions be reduced. They have taken part in meetings at the United Nations, and hold workshops and run campaigns for young islanders.

Pacific Climate Warriors representative Lisa Sipaia-Baker speaks to a crowd during a demonstration.

Soil and Land

Earth is made up of rock. Over millions of years the rock breaks down into soil, in which plants can grow, and insects, worms and burrowing animals can live.

We all need healthy soil. Humans rely on plants, or crops, grown in healthy soils for food, grass for feeding animals, cotton and other materials to make clothes, and timber for building.

MARVELLOUS SOIL

Soil is home to more than half of all life on Earth. One teaspoon of soil can contain more than a billion microorganisms!

The health of soil directly affects the health of plants grown in it and indirectly affects the health of animals who rely on those plants.

Some rocks and minerals are important in the fight against climate change and the shift to renewable energy. For instance, some metals and minerals are needed to make solar panels and electric batteries.

But other materials, such as coal and oil, should stay in the ground. Most countries are trying to reduce and eventually stop using coal and oil in favour of renewable energy such as solar and wind.

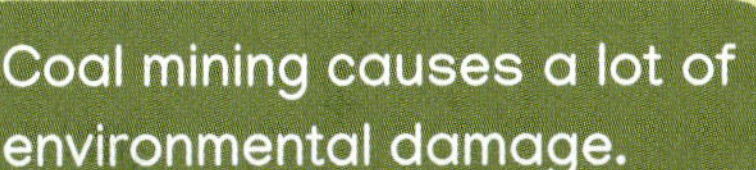
Coal mining causes a lot of environmental damage.

The use of renewable energy, including solar panels and wind turbines, is increasing worldwide.

When trees are cut down to make room for farms, cities and suburbs, the top layer of soil wears away. This is called "soil erosion".

Fertilisers and chemicals used to keep pests away from crops have also made soil less healthy.

These are serious problems for farmers, as crops won't grow well in poor soil. But there are many things we can do to protect soil. This includes planting in particular ways to avoid soil washing away, and using natural products such as compost or animal manure rather than fertilisers.

These children are learning how to grow plants well without using fertililsers.

YOUNG ENVIRONMENTAL HEROES:

Seed Mob

> A just and sustainable future ... powered by renewable energy.

Seed Mob is Australia's first Indigenous youth-led climate movement. In 2018 they made a film called *Water Is Life* about the dangers of **fracking** and the impact of such activities on bush foods in the Northern Territory. They have also campaigned against mining in traditional lands.

For members of Seed Mob, protecting their lands against climate change means protecting their future.

Seed Mob are working to try to prevent fracking in the Fitzroy River in the Kimberley, Western Australia. Fracking can bring contaminated water back to the water's surface, risking overflow of the river.

Living Things

Living things include all plants, animals and microorganisms. Healthy and diverse living communities are essential, as they provide us with food and other useful materials. The varied beauty of the natural world is also something most people want to conserve for the future.

Over the last 200 years, human activities have resulted in plant and animal habitats being destroyed. Fishing and hunting have made many species endangered or extinct. Forests have been cut down for farmland, logging or to build towns and cities. This means there are fewer trees to absorb the increasing carbon dioxide in the air.

Logging can destroy the habitats of many creatures and change the local environment.

Living things play a very important role in the environment, just like air, soil and water. For example, bees **pollinate** the fruit and vegetable plants that we grow to eat. Without bees, you would not have all the delicious fruits you love, such as strawberries and apples!

Bees are an essential part of our environment.

The use of chemical **insecticide** sprays is threatening the survival of honeybees. Climate change is also affecting bees because on hot days they do not pollinate plants. More hot days means less pollination.

To look after living things, we must protect and preserve **biodiversity**. This involves lots of different actions, including restoring natural habitats, protecting vulnerable species, and educating people about the importance of looking after the balance of nature.

By protecting the habitat of the western pygmy possum, we can help to prevent it from becoming extinct.

Trees

There are over 3 trillion trees on Earth. That's a lot – more than the number of stars in the Milky Way – but 10 billion trees are cut down every year!

YOUNG ENVIRONMENTAL HERO:

Lina Nayel Al-Tarawneh

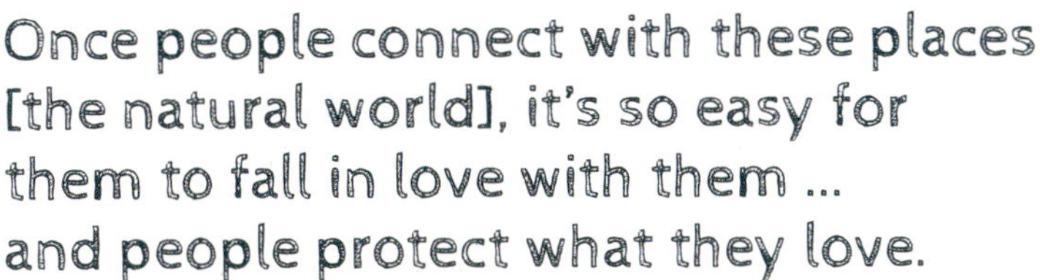

> "Once people connect with these places [the natural world], it's so easy for them to fall in love with them ... and people protect what they love."

Lina Nayel Al-Tarawneh is a young Muslim climate **activist** from Jordan.

Lina fell in love with the natural world on a camping trip with her family to an island in the Arabian Gulf. However, she was alarmed by the amount of rubbish she saw polluting the **mangroves** along the shoreline. She decided to do something about it. Lina bought some kayaks and set up Green Mangroves, an organisation that coordinates volunteers to clean up the mangroves. It also promotes the **conservation** of landscapes like these through education programs.

Mangroves like these in the Arabian Gulf are unique environments that can be easily damaged by pollution.

What Can I Do?

Thousands of young people are helping to protect our environment – and you can, too! Here are some ways you can make a difference.

Reduce, Reuse, Recycle

Reduce waste by avoiding buying things with lots of packaging. Use reusable and recyclable things such as cloth shopping bags. Lots of fossil fuels are needed to make plastics, so the less plastic we use, the better it is for our environment.

Make sure you put each type of rubbish in the right bin and make compost from your food waste.

Having different bins for different kinds of materials makes it easier to recycle.

Conserve Energy

Save energy by turning off lights, TVs and other electronics when you are not using them. Talk to your family and friends about switching to renewable energy sources like solar and wind power. Use public transportation, walk or cycle to school instead of having your parents drive you.

Save Water

Take shorter showers, and don't leave the tap running while washing dishes. Collect rainwater to water your garden.

A timer can help you keep your showers shorter.

Read and Learn

Read about environmental issues and solutions, then encourage your teachers, family and friends to discuss climate change and the environment. You could plant a vegetable garden at school or at home, and grow some of your own food.

Volunteer

You might have a local environmental group that runs clean-up events, tree-planting activities or conservation projects. By volunteering, you can make a positive impact in your community.

These young volunteers are helping to plant trees.

Be Your Own Environmental Hero

By understanding how all aspects of our environment are important and how we can protect them, you can become an environmental hero, too. You can help your family, school and local community reduce their impact on the planet, and work towards a healthier and more secure future for all living things.

Remember, even small actions can be the start of big changes!

Taking part in clean-up days in your local community is a great way to help the environment.

Glossary

activists *(noun)*	people who are trying to raise awareness about a particular cause
advocating *(verb)*	supporting or promoting a particular cause
atmosphere *(noun)*	the layer of gases around Earth
biodiversity *(noun)*	the variety of life on Earth
climate change *(noun)*	changes in weather patterns from a rise in Earth's temperature as a result of human activities, such as burning fossil fuels
conservation *(noun)*	protecting something, such as a particular environment
droughts *(noun)*	long periods with little to no rainfall
economic growth *(noun)*	increases in the value of goods and services or the overall wealth of a country or region
emissions *(noun)*	gases discharged into the atmosphere
equator *(noun)*	an imaginary circle around Earth
fertilisers *(noun)*	substances added to soil to help plants grow
fossil fuels *(noun)*	substances like petrol, oil or gas that are formed from the remains of things that lived a long time ago
fracking *(noun)*	a technology for getting gas or oil out of underground rock by drilling deep wells
ice caps *(noun)*	a thick layer of ice and snow over a large area
insecticide *(noun)*	a chemical mixture used to kill insects
mangroves *(noun)*	trees or bushes that grow in thick clusters beside the sea or along rivers
microorganisms *(noun)*	living things that are too small to be seen with our eyes alone
movement *(noun)*	a group of people who take action about the same issue or cause
pollinate *(verb)*	to carry pollen from one plant to another, allowing it to reproduce
sewage *(noun)*	liquid waste from toilets
solar panels *(noun)*	panels that convert sunlight into energy
ultraviolet (UV) light *(noun)*	a type of light that can damage or kill living cells
United Nations *(noun)*	an international organisation that promotes peace between different nations
water vapour *(noun)*	water in the form of a gas

Index